STATE & LOCAL GOVERNMENT

Troll Associates

STATE & LOCAL GOVERNMENT

by Laurence Santrey

Illustrated by Bob Dole

Troll Associates

Library of Congress Cataloging in Publication Data

Santrey, Laurence.
   State and local government.

   Summary: Discusses the development of state and local
government and their relationship to each other and to
the federal government.
   1. State governments—Juvenile literature.   2. Local
government—United States—Juvenile literature.
[1. State governments.   2. Local government]   I. Dole,
Bob, ill.   II. Title.
JK2408.S23   1985   353.9   84-8440
ISBN 0-8167-0270-5 (lib. bdg.)
ISBN 0-8167-0271-3 (pbk.)

After the thirteen American Colonies won their independence from Great Britain, they joined together as one nation. But they didn't give up their identities completely. Instead, the thirteen Colonies became thirteen states. And the Constitution of the new United States of America made sure that these identities would never be lost. It said that all powers not given to the federal government by the Constitution belong to the states or the people.

This was done because the founding fathers believed that any government with too much power could be dangerous. It might become a tyranny, like the British rule they had recently escaped. So they kept a great deal of government power for the states and for the people in them.

As each new state entered the Union, it was given the same powers as all the others. One of these powers is to make laws governing all matters within the state.

For example, the state of New York has its own code of criminal laws. These laws say how long a person convicted of a crime in New York will serve in prison for that crime. The state of New Jersey, the state of Utah, and each other state has its own code of criminal laws. These may set the same prison terms as neighboring states for crimes committed in their states. Or they may set prison terms that are very different from the other states.

But no state may make a law that inter-
feres with the business of any other state.
The Mississippi River, for instance, runs
between Missouri and Illinois. But neither
Illinois nor Missouri may make laws that
limit the use of the river to its own citizens.
Any time two or more states are involved, as
in this case, the federal government makes
the laws.

Every state must respect the laws of every other state. Suppose a man and woman get married in the state of Oregon. Their marriage is then legal in every one of the fifty states. And a person who is licensed to drive a motor vehicle in the state of New Mexico is legally allowed to drive in every other state in the Union.

Most countries in the world are divided into smaller units. These units may be called provinces, shires, counties, or departments. Or they may be called states, as they are in the United States of America. But there is a difference between the states of the United States and the units in most other countries.

In most of the countries, the national government makes all the laws. There are governors, mayors, and other local officials in these countries. But these officials just see that their laws are carried out.

In the United States, each unit, called a state, makes many of the laws that govern that state. And the officials do more than simply enforce laws made by the federal government in Washington.

The states of the United States are also divided into smaller units. These are called counties, cities, towns, townships, or districts. But these small units are not given any special powers by the Constitution. They have only the powers given to them by the states in which they exist. And a state may change the number of counties in it, as well as decide what the county governments or city governments may or may not do.

Each state government—just like the federal government—is made up of three branches, called the executive, the legislative, and the judicial branches. In the federal government, the President is head of the executive branch. In the state government, the governor is head of the executive branch.

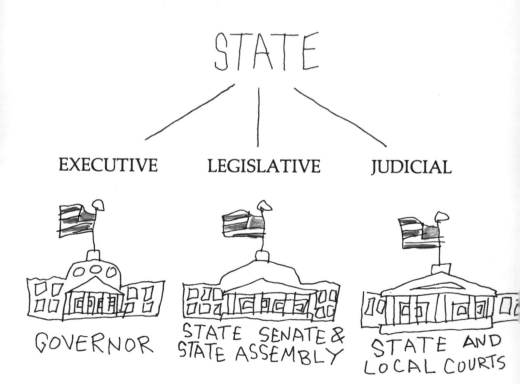

STATE

EXECUTIVE   LEGISLATIVE   JUDICIAL

GOVERNOR   STATE SENATE & STATE ASSEMBLY   STATE AND LOCAL COURTS

The legislative branch of the federal government is made up of two bodies, called the House of Representatives and the Senate. Forty-nine of the states also have two legislative bodies, usually called the state assembly and the state senate. Only the state of Nebraska has a one-house legislature.

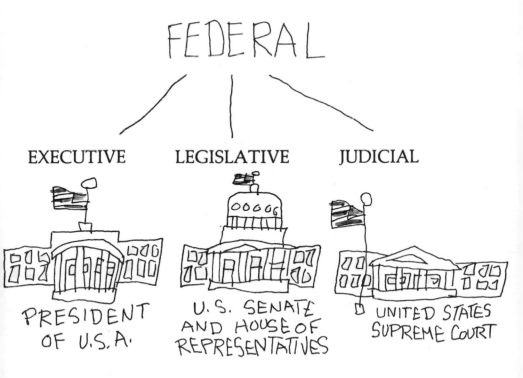

FEDERAL

EXECUTIVE   LEGISLATIVE   JUDICIAL

PRESIDENT OF U.S.A.   U.S. SENATE AND HOUSE OF REPRESENTATIVES   UNITED STATES SUPREME COURT

The Supreme Court of the United States and a number of lower courts make up the federal judiciary branch. At the state level there are also a number of courts. These state courts deal with a wide variety of legal matters. In fact, most law cases are decided in state courts. And just as the United States Constitution is the law for the whole country, there is a separate state constitution for each state.

The United States Constitution says what things a state cannot do. States cannot make treaties with foreign countries. They cannot make their own coins or paper money. They cannot put a tax on incoming or outgoing goods. And they cannot secede from the Union and become independent countries.

Even so, the states have great powers. Most of our day-to-day lives are governed by state laws. For example, each state runs its own school systems. It has its own criminal and civil laws. It licenses businesses, has its own motor-vehicle regulations, maintains its own police, and so on.

Here's how your state affects your daily life. Suppose you ride a bus to school. The bus must meet state standards and must be registered with the state. The bus driver is licensed by the state. The traffic regulations the driver obeys are set by the state. The school you attend must meet state standards for safety and health. The educational standards of your school are set by the state. The lunch room serves meals approved by the state and is inspected by state inspectors. Your teacher and principal and librarian are licensed by the state.

Suppose you have an after-school appointment with a doctor or dentist. That doctor or dentist is licensed to practice in the state. The nurse and the dental hygienist are also licensed by the state.

If you telephone a classmate in the eve-
ning, the cost of the call is approved by the
state and includes state taxes. And when you
turn on the lights at night, you are using
electricity that comes from a company that is
licensed and regulated by the state. So you
can see how important a part the state plays
in your everyday life.

The laws and regulations having to do with police, education, health, highways, and other state services are made by the state legislature. Each state legislature is elected by the voters of that state. Each state's constitution says how long a legislator's term will last. In some states, the terms are four years. In others, they are longer or shorter.

The governor of a state is also elected by the voters. The usual term of office is four years. In some states, a governor may not serve two terms in a row. In other states, there is no limit to how many consecutive terms a governor may serve.

The governor of each state has a cabinet made up of advisors on different matters. Some states have a lieutenant governor. A lieutenant governor is the second-highest executive official in the state.

Most states also have a treasurer, an attorney general (who is the state's highest lawyer), and other officials, who run many different departments. For example, there is

usually a state commissioner of education, a commissioner of health, a commissioner of police, and so forth.

The counties, cities, and other units within a state also have officials who serve the people. Counties are usually governed by elected supervisors or commissioners. Towns and cities often have an elected mayor and local legislature, called the city council or town council.

The mayor is the chief executive of the

city. The mayor sees that necessary local laws are passed and that they are carried out. The mayor also supervises the people who run different city departments.

The city council is something like the state legislature or the United States Congress—but on a much smaller scale. The city council makes the laws for the city.

The state gives different responsibilities to counties and cities. For example, counties and cities are responsible for some of the roads, for garbage collection, water supply, parks and recreation, libraries, local police, and so forth. To pay for these services, counties and cities receive tax money from the state and federal governments. They may also raise funds through taxes on property, water usage, garbage collection, and various business licenses.

Some large cities, such as New York, Chicago, San Francisco, and Boston, provide their citizens with a broad range of public services. They have city hospitals, city colleges and universities, public-transportation systems, and social-service systems to help children, old people, and the needy.

Small towns, villages, and farm areas don't usually offer all these public services. That is because they do not have a population large enough to use the services, or enough tax money to pay for them.

The United States is a very large and complex country. It has millions of citizens, countless miles of highways and telephone lines, and a huge array of products and industries.

Governing a country like this is not easy. No single level of government could handle it alone. But the partnership of national, state, and local governments gets the job done—efficiently, effectively, and for the benefit of everyone.